Derek
Jeter

By Mike Kennedy

Gareth Stevens
Publishing

Please visit our web site at www.garethstevens.com.
For a free catalog describing Gareth Stevens Publishing's list of high-quality books,
call 1-800-542-2595 (USA) or 1-800-387-3178 (Canada).
Gareth Stevens Publishing's fax: 1-877-542-2596

Library of Congress Cataloging-in-Publishing Data
Kennedy, Mike (Mike William), 1965–
    Derek Jeter / by Mike Kennedy.
        p. cm.— (Today's superstars)
    Includes bibliographical references and index.
    IISBN-10: 1-4339-1969-9   ISBN-13: 978-1-4339-1969-5 (lib. bdg.)
    ISBN-10: 1-4339-2162-6   ISBN-13: 978-1-4339-2162-9 (soft cover)
    1. Jeter, Derek, 1974– —Juvenile literature. 2. Baseball players—United States—Biography
Juvenile literature. I. Title.
    GV865.J48K46   2010
    796.357092—dc22 [B]   2009002540

This edition first published in 2010 by
Gareth Stevens Publishing
A Weekly Reader® Company
1 Reader's Digest Road
Pleasantville, NY 10570-7000 USA

Executive Managing Editor: Lisa M. Herrington
Senior Designer: Keith Plechaty

Produced by Editorial Directions, Inc.
Art Direction and Page Production: The Design Lab

Photo credits: cover, title page John A. Angelillo/Corbis; p. 4, 46 AP Photo/Amy Sancetta; p. 6 AP
Photo/Tony Dejak; p. 7 AP Photo/Doug Mills; p. 8 AP Photo/Amy Sancetta; p. 9 sabri deniz kizil/
Shutterstock; p. 10 AP Photo/Nick Wass; p. 12 Danny E Hooks/Shutterstock; p. 13 Jim McIsaac/
Getty Images; p. 14 Getty Images for Steiner Sports; p. 15 Yearbook Library; p. 16 Barbara Jean
Germano/WR; p. 18 Jim Rogash/Getty Images; p. 19 US Presswire/Zuma Press; p. 20 Barbara Jean
Germano/WR; p. 21 AP Photo/Ricardo Figueroa; p. 22, 40 John Klein/WR; p. 24 AP Photo/Mark
Lennihan; p. 25 Timothy A. Clary/AFP/Getty Images; p. 26, 41 Getty Images; p. 27 James Devaney/
WireImage; p. 28 AP Photo/Mark Lennihan; p. 30 AP Photo/Kalamazoo Gazette, Jonathon Gruenke;
p. 31 AP Photo/Ron Frehm; p. 32 Ciniglio Lorenzo/Corbis Sygma; p. 33 AP Photo/Eric Risberg; p. 34
Al Bello/Getty Images; p. 36 Mike Segar/Reuters/Corbis; p. 38 AP Photo/Gene J. Puskar; p. 39 AP
Photo/Julie Jacobson; p. 44 Trinicria Photo/Shutterstock

Printed in the United States of America

1 2 3 4 5 6 7 8 9 14 13 12 11 10 09

Contents

Words in the glossary appear in **bold** type the first time they are used in the text.

"I've never hit a walk-off home run before, SO IT WAS PRETTY SPECIAL."

—Derek Jeter

Jeter watches his game-winning home run in Game 4 of the 2001 World Series.

Chapter 1

Mr. November

Derek Jeter settled into the batter's box. The clock had just struck midnight. The calendar no longer read October 31. For the first time in history, the World Series was being played in November.

That year, the World Series had a late start. Only a few weeks before, the people of New York City had been devastated by the terrorist attacks of September 11, 2001. The baseball season was delayed as the country took time to recover.

The Yankees gave the people of New York a reason to celebrate. The team advanced through the playoffs and then reached the World Series. Now the sell-out crowd at Yankee Stadium buzzed as their star player stepped up to bat.

All About Derek

Name: Derek Sanderson Jeter

Birth date: June 26, 1974

Birthplace: Pequannock, New Jersey

Height: 6 feet 3 inches (191 centimeters)

Weight: 195 pounds (88 kilograms)

Current homes: New York, New York; Tampa, Florida

Family: Parents Dorothy and Charles; sister Sharlee

Fact File

Hall of Famer Reggie Jackson is known as Mr. October for his great record in the playoffs and World Series with the Yankees.

Right Time, Right Place

Jeter didn't look the least bit nervous. Yankee fans knew they had the right guy at the plate. They were used to seeing the All-Star shortstop do amazing things under pressure.

And the pressure was definitely on. The New York Yankees were hosting the Arizona Diamondbacks in Game 4 of the 2001 World Series. The score was tied 3–3 in the bottom of the 10th inning. There were two outs, and the count on Jeter was three balls and two strikes.

Over and Out

Jeter waited for the next pitch. He loved being in this type of situation. He always seemed to get a hit or make a great play in the field when his team needed it most.

This time was no exception. Jeter watched the ball leave the pitcher's hand and curve as it crossed home plate. Jeter took a swing and launched a high fly ball to right field. The soaring drive cleared the fence for a home run. The Yankees won 4–3! "I've never hit a **walk-off home run** before, so it was pretty special," Jeter said.

TRUE OR FALSE?

Jeter was the first Yankee to hit a walk-off home run in the World Series.

For answers, see page 46.

Playoff Hero

Jeter is one of the best **postseason** players in baseball history. From 1996 to 2003, he led the Yankees to the World Series (also known as the "Fall Classic") six times. New York won the championship four times. Jeter was named the Most Valuable Player (MVP) of the 2000 World Series when the Yankees beat the New York Mets. Through 2008, he holds several postseason records, including most hits (153) and most runs (85).

◀ Jeter celebrates a grand slam by teammate Tino Martinez during the 1998 World Series.

A Special Feeling

Jeter's game-winning homer set off a huge celebration. Yankee Stadium erupted in cheers. Yankee fans everywhere jumped for joy. They called him Mr. November.

"When I first hit it I had no idea [it was a home run]," Jeter said after the game. "But once it goes out, it's a pretty special feeling."

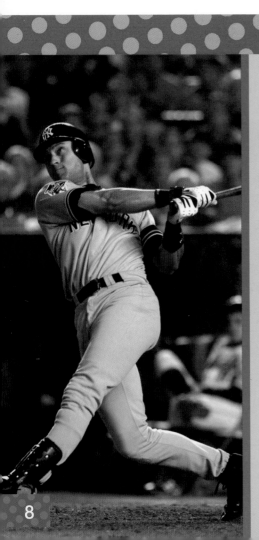

Beyond the Numbers

Jeter's lifetime batting average is far above .300. He made the All-Star team for the ninth time in 2008. He led the Yankees to the playoffs in each of his first 12 seasons. Statistics, however, aren't the best way to define Jeter. Just ask Joe Torre. He was the manager of the Yankees when Jeter broke into the major leagues. With Torre calling the shots from the dugout and Jeter leading the team in the field, the Yankees won the World Series four times. Torre credits Jeter for much of the team's success. "It seems when something needs to happen," Torre says, "[Jeter is] at the start of it or the finish of it."

◀ Jeter launches a home run during Game 5 of the 2000 World Series.

1 Number of times Jeter struck out during his senior season in high school

2 Jeter's uniform number

97 Jeter's RBI (runs batted in) total during the 2006 season

138 Number of times Jeter was hit by pitches in his first 12 seasons

219 Number of hits Jeter had in 1999 to lead the American League

$21.6 million Jeter's salary in 2008

12:03 A.M. The time of Jeter's game-winning home run in Game 4 of the 2001 World Series

Team Spirit

Jeter's home run against the Diamondbacks is one of many thrilling moments in his incredible career. Since he first stepped on a baseball diamond, he has had a talent for coming through in the **clutch**. That's one of the many reasons why Yankees fans love him.

Is Jeter a perfect player? No. In fact, he is the first to admit this. Is he the ultimate team player? Absolutely. When the Yankees win, he's happy. When they lose, he's not. For him, that's when the real work starts.

Fact File

In addition to calling him Mr. November, Yankee fans have nicknamed Jeter Captain Clutch.

"My parents always said, 'If you work hard, **THEN YOU CAN DO IT.'**"

—Derek Jeter

Jeter leaps to make a throw to first base. As a kid, he dreamed of playing for the Yankees.

Chapter 2
Family Affair

Some kids know from an early age what they want to be when they grow up. Derek was one of those kids. He loved baseball and wanted to play professionally. In fact, in junior high school, he even predicted that he would one day be the shortstop for the Yankees.

Of course, Derek didn't make his dream come true by simply wishing it would happen. He was blessed with great talent, but he also worked hard and never backed down from a challenge. Where did he learn his winning ways? He credits his family with giving him the drive to succeed. "My parents always said, 'If you work hard, then you can do it.'"

Derek's Favorites

- ✔ **Athlete:** Michael Jordan
- ✔ **Moment of his career:** Winning the 1996 World Series
- ✔ **Subject in school:** Math
- ✔ **TV Shows:** *American Idol* and *Entourage*
- ✔ **College team:** University of Michigan Wolverines
- ✔ **Video game:** Ms. Pac-Man
- ✔ **Pizza topping:** Pepperoni

Jersey Boy

Derek Sanderson Jeter was born on June 26, 1974 in Pequannock, New Jersey. He was the first of two children. His sister, Sharlee, was born five years after Derek.

Sports were a big part of life in the Jeter home. Like his mother, Dorothy, and father, Charles, Derek was a huge baseball fan. His favorite team was the Yankees. His favorite player was All-Star outfielder Dave Winfield, who played for New York in the 1980s.

TRUE OR FALSE?

Charles Jeter was a pitcher on his college baseball team.

On the Move

When Derek was four, the Jeters moved to Kalamazoo, Michigan. Charles worked as a counselor for people addicted to drugs and alcohol. Dorothy was an accountant.

Derek's mom and dad were different from the parents of his friends. Dorothy is white, and Charles is black. Derek was sometimes teased because of his mixed racial background. Dorothy and Charles taught him to see past people's skin color.

Fact File

When Derek was 12, he met his favorite player—Dave Winfield—and got his autograph.

▲ Jeter poses for a picture with his mom, sister, and dad. Dorothy has been a big influence on his career.

Behind the Mask

When Derek was growing up, his mom was often the one who helped him work on his baseball skills. Dorothy knew a lot about the game, from hitting to fielding. Sometimes, she even put on a catcher's mask when he wanted to practice his pitching. As Derek got older, she continued to lend her support—and her advice—whenever her son needed it. That didn't end once Derek joined the Yankees. Dorothy has even helped him break out of batting slumps. As Jeter says today, "Usually her advice works."

Education First

In Michigan, Derek found lots of opportunities to play baseball. He started his career in Little League. He also gathered his friends from the neighborhood for **pickup games**.

Charles and Dorothy realized that Derek had a lot of talent. They encouraged him to pursue baseball—as long as he worked hard in school. If his grades dropped, he wasn't allowed to play.

▲ Sharlee accepts a check for Jeter's Turn 2 Foundation. She is an important part of her brother's life.

Best Friends

Derek and his sister, Sharlee, have always been close. They talk on the phone almost every day. When Sharlee was young, she was also a good athlete. Her best sport was softball, but she chose to give it up in college. She wanted to focus on her education. In November 2000, Sharlee was diagnosed with a form of cancer known as Hodgkin's disease. She survived and has remained cancer-free as of early 2009. "Now [she's] a success story," says Derek of his sister, who is one of his best friends.

School Days

Derek entered Kalamazoo Central High School in the fall of 1988. He was a good student and had a lot of friends. Derek also excelled in sports. He played guard on the school's basketball team. As a sophomore, he hit a long shot at the buzzer to beat rival Portage Central High School.

▲ Derek knew he wanted to be a major leaguer from the first day he suited up for Kalamazoo Central High School.

Derek was at his best on the baseball diamond. People compared him to Cal Ripken Jr., the star shortstop for the Baltimore Orioles. Derek could do it all. He was a great hitter, fielder, and base runner.

Pro **scouts** began showing up at Derek's games when he was a junior. That season, he batted .557 and slammed seven home runs. Before long, his dream of being a big leaguer would become reality.

Fact File

In youth basketball leagues, Derek played against future NBA stars Chris Webber and Jalen Rose.

"I always wanted to play baseball **IN THE MAJOR LEAGUES.**"

— Derek Jeter

Jeter gets ready for a pitch during his days with the Columbus Clippers. He spent four years in the minor leagues.

Chapter 3

Minor Adjustments

To get to the major leagues, most players have to go through the **minor leagues**. There they are taught the ins and outs of professional baseball. Life in the minors can be hard. Players travel from town to town on buses. They live in tiny apartments and eat a lot of fast food. They get homesick, go through batting slumps, and make errors in the field.

Derek Jeter went from high school directly to the minors. He struggled at times, but he learned from his mistakes. He decided that nothing was going to stop him from becoming a Yankee. "I always wanted to play baseball in the major leagues, praying the Yankees would be the team that drafted me," Jeter said.

Draft Dandies

The amateur baseball draft is held every June by teams in the major leagues. One by one, they take turns picking from the top players in college and high school. Stars are found everywhere from the draft's first round to its last round. Jeter was one of many stars selected early in the 1992 draft. Other major leaguers taken that year included Todd Helton, Raul Ibanez, and Jeter's future teammates Jason Giambi and Johnny Damon.

◀ Jeter celebrates with Johnny Damon. Both were selected in the 1992 draft.

Senior Year

Jeter's final season at Kalamazoo Central High School was an outstanding one, and he batted .508. After the season, Jeter was named the national High School Player of the Year.

Jeter faced a big decision. He wanted to start his professional career as soon as possible. However, the University of Michigan had offered him a baseball **scholarship**. He talked things over with his parents. They agreed that he should follow his dream and go pro.

Fact File

Jeter plans to get his college degree once his baseball career is over.

Up and Down

After Jeter turned pro, he waited to see which team would take him in the 1992 draft. He wanted to play for the Yankees, but other teams were interested. Derek celebrated when New York called his name with the sixth pick in the first round.

A few weeks later, Jeter joined the Yankees' minor-league team in Tampa, Florida. He was soon promoted to a minor-league team in Greensboro, North Carolina. But he struggled. Jeter struck out 16 times in 11 games. In the field, he flubbed easy grounders and made bad throws to first base. He was disappointed in his play but determined to improve.

▶ Jeter's first stop in the minors was with the Tampa Yankees.

19

On the Rise

For the 1993 season, Jeter was back in Greensboro. He worked hard on his swing and raised his batting average. But he made 56 errors at shortstop. He talked to his parents and got advice from his coaches. They helped him stay positive.

Jeter began to show his true form in 1994. For the season, he hit .344, stole 50 bases, and made fewer mistakes in the field. *Baseball America*, *Baseball Weekly*, and *The Sporting News* all named him the Minor League Player of the Year.

No Place Like Home

Like many minor leaguers, Jeter got homesick during his first few years in the minors. He wasn't used to being away from his family. When Jeter didn't play well, he worried that his dream of reaching the majors might not come true. He often called home for words of encouragement. In his first season, Jeter's phone bills were about $300 a month.

◀ Jeter smiles for a picture for the Columbus Clippers. But his time in the minors wasn't always happy.

Friend to the End

One of Jeter's best friends is teammate Jorge Posada. They share a lot in common. The two met in 1994, when they played in the minors for Columbus. Both were up-and-coming stars, and both hated to lose. Jeter and Posada brought a winning attitude to the Yankees. Heading into the 2009 season, they had played next to each other for 15 years. When Posada got married in 2000, Jeter was his best man. "He's very, very special," says Posada. "It's tough not to like him."

◀ Posada and Jeter share a laugh at Posada's wedding.

Ready for the Big Time

Jeter played the 1995 season as if he had something to prove. In reality, he did. He wanted to show the Yankees that he was ready for the majors. They took notice.

Jeter opened the year with New York's minor-league team in Columbus, Ohio. He sizzled at the plate, hitting well above .300. In the field, he was smooth and effortless. Jeter also developed into a leader who encouraged his teammates. The Yankees realized that they had a special player.

Fact File

Jeter made it to the majors for the first time in 1995. He played 15 games for the Yankees that year.

> ## "Nothing has stopped him.
>
> ## HE SEEMS TO CONQUER EVERYTHING IN A VERY COOL WAY."
>
> —Yankees owner George Steinbrenner

Jeter lines a hit during his rookie season. He amazed teammates and fans with his great performance that year.

Chapter 4

Major Accomplishments

Normally, making the leap from the minor leagues to the major leagues is very difficult. The competition is stiffer, the crowds are bigger, and the pressure to win is more intense. Young players often struggle during their first year or two.

Jeter, however, never skipped a beat. He worked hard every day in practice. He asked more experienced teammates for advice. He listened to every instruction given by his coaches. From his first day in the majors, the **rookie** looked like he belonged. Yankees owner George Steinbrenner would later say of Jeter, "Nothing has stopped him. He seems to conquer everything in a very cool way."

THE KID CATCHES ON AS NEW YANKEE HERO

▲ Jeffrey Maier found himself in the national spotlight after catching Jeter's home run ball.

A Helping Hand

Jeter hit one of baseball's most famous home runs in Game 1 of the 1996 **American League Championship Series**. But was it really a home run? With New York losing 4–3 in the bottom of the eighth inning, Jeter launched a high drive to right field in Yankee Stadium. A young fan named Jeffrey Maier reached over the fence and snagged the ball. The Baltimore Orioles argued, but the umpires ruled it a home run. The Yankees won in 11 innings.

TRUE OR FALSE?

Jeter hit a home run in his first at-bat on opening day in 1996.

Remarkable Rookie

For the 1996 season, Yankees manager Joe Torre made Jeter the starting shortstop. Jeter batted .314 for the year and played great defense. He was an easy choice as American League Rookie of the Year.

He was even better in the playoffs. In the 1996 American League Championship Series, Jeter hit .417 and made a diving stop for the last out of the series. The Yankees moved on to the World Series and beat the Atlanta Braves in six games.

Season for the Ages

Jeter had another great season in 1997, but the Yankees were unable to repeat as World Series champions. New York returned to the top of baseball the following year. The team set a record with 114 wins during the regular season. They advanced to the World Series and swept the San Diego Padres in four games.

Once again, Jeter was key to New York's success. He led the American League with 127 runs scored. For the first time, he was named to the All-Star team. In the World Series, he batted .353.

Fact File

In 1997, Tim Raines, Derek Jeter, and Paul O'Neill became the first Yankees to hit back-to-back-to-back home runs in the playoffs.

▼ Jeter gets a high five from manager Joe Torre after a win by the Yankees.

Repeat Performance

After the Yankees' amazing 1998 season, their fans were hungry for another World Series championship. Jeter and his teammates delivered. In 1999, the team battled injuries all year long but never panicked. The Yankees beat the Braves again in the World Series.

As usual, Jeter proved to be New York's leader. He finished second in the league with a .349 batting average and knocked in more than 100 runs for the first time. In the playoffs, he came through in the clutch time and again.

▼ Jeter tags out Otis Nixon during the 1999 World Series. The Yankees swept the Braves in four games.

Leading Man

In New York, Jeter is always in the spotlight. That's true even off the field. Jeter's good looks and athletic ability make him one of the sports world's most eligible single men. He has been linked to Mariah Carey, Jessica Biel, Jessica Alba, and Vanessa Minnillo. Jeter thinks the rumors spread about him are more interesting than his real life. As he once said, "It's amazing the things that are in the gossip pages. They've got me dating everyone imaginable."

◀ Jeter sits courtside with Vanessa Minnillo during a New York Knicks game.

Star Power

In just three years in New York, Jeter had become a superstar. Yankee fans adored him. The team signed him to a contract worth millions of dollars. He never wanted to play for another team.

Jeter enjoyed the attention and was grateful for the money. But he wasn't satisfied. The Yankees had won the World Series three times in four years. He wanted another championship.

TRUE OR FALSE?

Jeter was the first rookie to start at shortstop for the Yankees in team history.

"Second place has never **REALLY SETTLED IN WITH ME.**"

—Derek Jeter

Winning is the bottom line for Jeter. He is at his best when his team needs him the most.

Chapter 5
New York's Finest

What makes a truly great player? One thing is the desire to improve. That's why Jeter works so hard. He knows that there's always something extra he can do to help his team win.

Great players also love the pressure of the big game. In fact, they thrive under it. Jeter understands this better than anyone. He saves his best for the most important moments. "You want to be the best you can be, individually and as a team. Second place has never really settled in with me," Jeter has said.

The 2000 season was a challenging one for the Yankees. Injuries forced manager Joe Torre to juggle his lineup and use many different players. Torre knew Jeter would play his best no matter what.

Making a Difference

Jeter uses his fame to help others. In 1996, he started the Turn 2 Foundation. Today, the foundation has grown to become a great success. It helps kids steer clear of drugs and alcohol, and it sponsors academic scholarships. It also holds baseball clinics that teach kids how to play the game, and it promotes physical fitness. Turn 2 has raised more than $8 million since it was created.

▲ **Jeter meets with a young fan. He enjoys being a role model for children.**

Fact File

In 2000, Jeter became the first Yankee to be named All-Star MVP.

All-Star Story

Sometimes Jeter was the team's **leadoff hitter**. Other times, he batted second or third. In the All-Star Game, Torre put Jeter in the starting lineup after Alex Rodriguez got hurt.

Jeter took advantage of his All-Star opportunity. He batted second and went 3-for-3 with two runs batted in. He helped the American League to a 6–3 victory over the National League. Jeter's performance was so impressive that he was named the game's MVP.

Subway Series

Jeter's great performance in the All-Star Game set the stage for the rest of the season. The Yankees won their division and then rolled through the American League playoffs. New York advanced to the World Series for the third year in a row. Their opponent was one of their biggest rivals, the crosstown New York Mets.

The mood in New York City was electric. Fans of the Yankees and Mets could barely wait for the first pitch of the "Subway Series." Jeter felt the same way. It was his time to shine again.

Fact File

In 2001, Jeter became the first Yankee to hit a home run in the All-Star Game since Yogi Berra in 1959.

▼ Jeter (center) joins the celebration after New York's 2000 American League championship.

▼ Jeter receives a key to the city from New York City mayor Rudy Giuliani after the Yankees' World Series victory in 2000.

Toast of the Town

The World Series was a dream come true for Yankees fans—and a nightmare for Mets supporters. In Game 1, Jeter threw out a runner at the plate to save a run. The Yankees went on to win 4–3 in 12 innings. In the next game, Jeter collected three hits in another victory.

Jeter was just warming up. He opened Game 4 with a home run. Later, he hit a triple and scored the winning run in a 3–2 victory. The following night, Jeter homered again. The Yankees won the World Series, and Jeter was voted MVP.

▲ Jeter watches Jorge Posada tag out Jeremy Giambi. The Yankees beat the A's thanks to their great teamwork.

Backup Plan

In the 2001 playoffs against the Oakland A's, Jeter made a defensive play that fans and sportscasters still talk about. The Yankees were leading in Game 3. Oakland's Jeremy Giambi was on first base, and Terrence Long hit a double to right field. Giambi raced around third base, heading for home plate. The throw from the outfield bounced wildly toward the infield. Out of nowhere, Jeter grabbed the ball and flipped it to Jorge Posada. The New York catcher tagged out Giambi, and the Yankees went on to win 1–0.

November Magic

Jeter's next World Series highlight was his home run against Arizona in 2001. This time, however, the Yankees didn't win the Fall Classic. Their championship run was stopped by the Diamondbacks, who won the series in seven games. New York fans cheered their team anyway.

Jeter was happy to see the people of New York City bounce back from the attacks of 9/11. Jeter was proud to give them something to feel good about.

Fact File

Jeter hosted *Saturday Night Live* in December 2001. He also appeared as himself in the 1990s sitcom *Seinfeld* and in the movie *Anger Management*.

"It's simple if you look at it as: **TRY TO WIN.**"

—Derek Jeter

As captain of the Yankees, Jeter is the team leader on and off the field.

Chapter 6
"C" Is for Captain

Leading a championship team is a tough job. Jeter has experienced that firsthand. Even winning teams suffer through rough spots. Hitters go into slumps. Pitchers have trouble throwing strikes. Managers sometimes don't make the right decisions. Jeter has always helped his teammates pull it together when they face a challenge.

What's even tougher is leading a team that falls short of expectations. Fans grow impatient. Reporters and sportscasters drum up controversy. Players get frustrated. Jeter knows what that is like, too. His leadership skills have been tested on many occasions. In these situations, he relies on his work ethic and winning attitude to lift his team. "It's simple if you look at it as: Try to win," he says.

Down but Not Out

Jeter will do anything to win. His dedication was on full display in a game against the Boston Red Sox during the 2004 season. The score was tied 3–3 in the top of the 12th inning. Two runners were on base. Boston's Trot Nixon hit a short fly down the left field line. At the crack of the bat, Jeter raced after the ball. He snagged the pop-up for the third out—and then crashed headfirst into the stands. Jeter walked off the field with a black eye and blood trickling down his face. The Yankees won two innings later, 5–4.

▲ Jeter is upside down, and New York fans jump for joy after his amazing catch against the Red Sox.

In 2002, *The Sporting News* honored Jeter as the "Good Guy in Sports" for his work to help people in the community.

Taking Charge

The Yankees hoped to regain their championship form in the 2002 season. Though the roster was filled with new players, the team won its division. Jeter did his part, especially in the playoffs. He batted .500 and hit two home runs against the Anaheim Angels. It wasn't enough. New York lost in the **Division Series** in four games.

Playing Through Pain

The next year, the Yankees honored Jeter by naming him team captain. But that season got off to a rough start. In a game against the Toronto Blue Jays, he suffered a painful separated shoulder. He was out of the lineup for six weeks. When he returned, his shoulder still bothered him.

Despite his injury, Jeter finished the 2003 season with a .324 batting average. It was third-best in the league. The Yankees followed their leader to another division title. New York returned to the World Series but lost to the Florida Marlins.

Fact File

Jeter hosts an annual celebrity golf tournament in Florida that raises thousands of dollars for charity.

Where Jeter Ranks

Babe Ruth. Lou Gehrig. Joe DiMaggio. Yogi Berra. Mickey Mantle. Some of baseball's greatest hitters have worn Yankee pinstripes. Is Jeter the next legend? Here's how he ranks on some all-time team lists through 2008:

Jeter's Stats	Jeter's Rank	Current Leader
Batting Average: .316	5th	Babe Ruth (.349)
Runs: 1,467	4th	Babe Ruth (1,959)
Hits: 2,535	2nd	Lou Gehrig (2,721)
Doubles: 411	5th	Lou Gehrig (534)
Stolen Bases: 275	2nd	Rickey Henderson (326)

▼ **Jeter chats with Alex
Rodriguez during
spring training in 2009.**

Room for Two

In 2004, the Yankees traded for shortstop Alex Rodriguez from the Texas Rangers. "A-Rod" moved from shortstop to third base, while Jeter kept his position. People thought the two superstars might not get along.

Rodriguez and Jeter both played well— and played as teammates. A-Rod was named the American League MVP in 2005 and 2007. Jeter played in four All-Star Games and won three **Gold Gloves**. The Yankees made the playoffs each year from 2004 to 2007. But Jeter and his teammates failed to reach the World Series.

▶ Jeter rounds the bases after hitting the home run that gave the Yankees their first win in their new stadium.

A Living Legend

After the 2008 season, Yankee Stadium closed its doors. The team opened a new Yankee Stadium in 2009. Fans had mixed feelings. Although the old stadium was run-down, it had great history.

After the final game at the old Yankee Stadium, Jeter addressed the crowd. "There are a few things with the Yankees that never change," he said. "Pride, tradition, and most of all, we have the greatest fans in the world."

With that, Yankees fans cheered loudly and proudly. They realized they were watching another great moment in the career of a Yankees legend.

TRUE OR FALSE?

Jeter had the most hits in the 85-year history of old Yankee Stadium.

Time Line

1974 Derek Jeter is born on June 26 in Pequannock, New Jersey.

1978 The Jeters move to Kalamazoo, Michigan.

1988 Jeter makes the varsity basketball team at Kalamazoo Central High School.

1992 Jeter is drafted by the Yankees.

1996 Jeter is named American League Rookie of the Year.

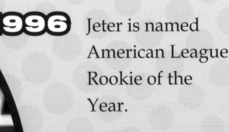

1998   Jeter leads the
Yankees to their
second World Series
in three years.

2000   Jeter is named World
Series MVP.

2003   Jeter is named captain of
the Yankees.

2004   Jeter wins his first
Gold Glove Award.

2008   Jeter makes his ninth
All-Star team.

Glossary

American League Championship Series: the best-of-seven playoff series that determines which team will represent the American League in the World Series

clutch: a difficult or critical situation

Division Series: the round of playoffs before each league's Championship Series. Each is a best-of-five format.

Gold Gloves: awards given each year for excellent fielding at each position in both the American and National leagues

leadoff hitter: the first hitter in a batting order

minor leagues: the many professional leagues below the major leagues. Players usually spend time in the minors learning more about the game before they move up to the majors.

pickup games: games played by neighborhood friends

postseason: games played after the regular season, in the playoffs and World Series

rookie: an athlete in his or her first season with a professional sports team

scholarship: a support program that provides funding for college and other educational pursuits

scouts: people whose job is to find young talented players for major league teams

walk-off home run: a home run hit by the home team that ends a game. After the home run, the players on the visiting team "walk off" the field.

To Find Out More

Books

Jeter, Derek, and Jack Curry. *The Life You Imagine: Life Lessons for Achieving Your Dreams.* New York: Crown Publishers, 2000.

Stewart, Mark. *The New York Yankees.* Chicago: Norwood House, 2007.

Stewart, Mark. *Ultimate 10: Clutch Performers.* Pleasantville, NY: Gareth Stevens, 2009.

Web Sites

JockBio.com: Derek Jeter
www.jockbio.com/Bios/Jeter/Jeter_bio.html
Find out biographical information, facts, and what others say about Jeter.

New York Yankees — Player File: Derek Jeter
http://mlb.mlb.com/team/player.jsp?player_id=116539
Get statistics and read the latest news about Jeter.

Turn 2 Foundation
http://derekjeter.mlb.com/players/jeter_derek/turn2/index.jsp
Learn more about Jeter's charitable organization.

Championships and Awards

American League Rookie of the Year
1996

World Series champion
1996, 1998, 1999, 2000

All-Star
1998, 1999, 2000, 2001, 2002, 2004, 2006, 2007, 2008

All-Star Game MVP
2000

World Series MVP
2000

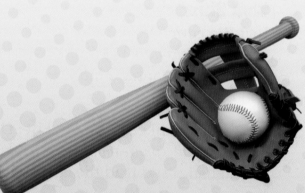

Gold Glove Award
2004, 2005, 2006

Silver Slugger Award
2006, 2007, 2008

American League Hank Aaron Award
2006

Source Notes

p. 7 Carrie Muskat, "Martinez, Jeter stun D-Back to even series," mlb.com, November 1, 2001.

p. 8 top Carrie Muskat.

p. 8 bottom Harvey Araton, "Sports of the Times; Jeter Is the Yankees' True Maximum Leader," *New York Times*, April 12, 2006.

p. 11 John Lowe, "Rookie Jeter Pleased in Pinstripes; Parents Watch Kalamazoo Shortstop Make Major Step With Yanks," Detroit *Free Press*, April 2, 1996.

p. 13 Liz Robbins, "BASEBALL; Jeter Is Looking for Hits at the End of the Tunnel," *New York Times*, May 11, 2000.

p. 14 Jack Curry, "BASEBALL; Jeter Shares the Success of Sister's Winning Fight," *New York Times*, May 13, 2001.

p. 17 Derek Jeter and Jack Curry, *The Life You Imagine: Life Lessons for Achieving Your Dreams*, New York, Crown Publishers, 2000.

p. 21 *New York Daily News*, July 4, 1999.

p. 23 Jon Heyman, "Kid Gloves – Steady Jeter, dazzling Ordonez make it summer of the rookie shortstops," *Newsday*, August 18, 1996.

p. 27 "Jeter watch goes from microscope to spotlight," ESPN.com news services, February 14, 2003.

p. 29 "Great Interview With Derek Jeter." Inside The Yankees blog, April 16, 2006. insidetheyankees.com/2006/04/great-interview-with-derek-jeter.html

p. 35 Tyler Kepner, "Jeter's Secret? It's Simple: Play to Win," *New York Times*, August 18, 2006.

p. 39 ESPN, September 21, 2008.

True or False Answers

Page 7   False. He was the fourth. The others were Chad Curtis (1999), Mickey Mantle (1964), and Tommy Henrich (1949).

Page 8   True. It is called Driven.

Page 12   False. Charles Jeter played shortstop at Fisk University in Nashville, Tennessee.

Page 14   False. A cousin, Gary Jeter, was a defensive lineman for the New York Giants football team.

Page 19   False. He was the third. The first two were Dennis Sherrill (1974) and Rex Hudler (1978).

Page 20   True. She loved Yankees player Dave Winfield, too.

Page 24   True.

Page 27   False. Rookie Tommy Tresh was New York's starting shortstop in 1962.

Page 32   True.

Page 39   True.

Jeter was the fourth Yankee to hit a walk-off homer in the World Series.

Index

About the Author

Mike Kennedy is a huge sports fan who has written dozens of books for kids. He has covered everything from the Super Bowl to skateboarding. Mike grew up in Ridgewood, New Jersey, and went to Franklin & Marshall College, where he earned letters in baseball and football. Today, Mike loves to run on trails and play golf. He and his wife, Ali, live in Boulder, Colorado. His favorite baseball team is the Yankees.